Spark and His Screenagains

By Mary Affee &
Lynn Louise Wonders

Illustrated by Ricky Audi

D1518771

Ormond Beach, FL
United States

Printed in the United States of America

Mary Affee's Dedication Message:
It's with joy, frustration, and lots of laughter I send this book out into the world to honor the time spent with my dear friends Adam Piper and Julia Krebs. I am reminded of the many countless hours we spent huddling in our small office with our very large dry erase board, as we created the blueprint for our screen time coaching project to help families create more connection and balance in their homes. I am thankful for you both.

Lynn Louise Wonders' Dedication Message:
Grateful Mary Affee invited me to join in this book project and many projects to come to help families and child therapists everywhere become more aware of the importance of reevaluating the amount of time we are all spending on our screens and invest more time playing, interacting and connecting face to face and outdoors.

Hi! I'm Spark! This is my house and this is my grassy yard. I love to play outside with my human family!

The problem is... ever since my human family became *screenagains* they never want to come out and play with me anymore.

This is the family room where the *screenagains* gather and stare at that big screen on the wall that shows moving pictures and makes lots of noise. When they stare at that big screen it's like they can't even see me or hear me!

This is our kitchen. When the *screenagains* sit at the table, they all stare at these small screens they hold in their hands and they don't even remember to share their snacks with me.

This is the big *screenagains'* room where they sleep. The big screenigans used to rub my belly and brush my fur.

Now, they are always staring at their screens all day and into the night. It's like they don't remember I am here.

I go outside and do my business. I sniff around. . .
but I feel sad because I have no one to play with me.

My human family used to play with me before and after school and work. But since they turned into *screenagains*, they don't pay any attention to me anymore.

I'm so happy! They look happy!
Let's play! Let's play!

Now that I have my humans back I know how to get them to come outside and play with me. I hope they remember how much fun we had today together outside without screens!

About the Authors

Dr. Mary Affee is the founder of Horizon Integrated Wellness Group, PLLC, in Cary, North Carolina, a practice that specializes in providing mental health services for children, teens and families. Mary is a licensed Clinical Social worker, and a Registered Play Therapist Supervisor. She is also an adjunct professor at Molloy College, where she teaches play therapy and expressive therapies in the school's Clinical Mental Health Counseling program. When she is not caring for her clients, Dr. Affee relishes time with her granddaughter, Adalina.

Lynn Louise Wonders is founder and director of Wonders Counseling Services, LLC in Ormond Beach, Florida. She is a licensed and certified professional counselor and has spent the last 20+ years supporting children and families, training therapists worldwide in play therapy and she is the author of the Miss Piper's Playroom children's book series.

Made in the USA
Middletown, DE
30 August 2022